EXPLORE IRAN
12 KEY FACTS

by Danielle Sovereign

www.12StoryLibrary.com

12-Story Library is an imprint of Bookstaves.

Photographs ©: Andrea Thompson Photography/Getty Images, cover, 1; Michal Knitl/Shutterstock.com, 4; Marcin Szymczak/Shutterstock.com, 5; Samane GH/Shutterstock.com, 6; Ted/CC2.0, 7; Royal Court of Iran/CC, 8; Frederic Legrand - COMEO/Shutterstock.com, 10; Zoheir Seidanloo/CC4.0, 11; anekoho/Shutterstock.com, 12; Chintung Lee/Shutterstock.com, 13; Grigvovan/Shutterstock.com, 14; Cordelia Persen/CC2.0, 15; Behnood Bandi/CC4.0, 16; Gorodenkoff/Shutterstock.com, 17; Borna_Mirahmadian/Shutterstock.com, 18; Grigvovan/Shutterstock.com, 19; Grigvovan/Shutterstock.com, 20; Marcin Szymczak/Shutterstock.com, 21; Zurijeta/Shutterstock.com, 22; bonchan/Shutterstock.com, 23; Zurijeta/Shutterstock.com, 24; Shabkhiz/CC4.0, 25; Leonid Andronov/Shutterstock.com, 26; Shahram Khorasanizadeh/Shutterstock.com, 27; Charlie Waradee/Shutterstock.com, 27; dovla982/Shutterstock.com, 28; Nannucci/iStockphoto, 29

ISBN
978-1-63235-556-0 (hardcover)
978-1-63235-612-3 (paperback)
978-1-63235-673-4 (ebook)

Library of Congress Control Number: 2018940817

Printed in the United States of America
Mankato, MN
June 2018

About the Cover

View of the tiled dome of the Imam Mosque in Esfahan, Iran. Completed in 1629, it is considered a masterpiece of Persian architecture.

Access free, up-to-date content on this topic plus a full digital version of this book. Scan the QR code on page 31 or use your school's login at 12StoryLibrary.com.

Table of Contents

Iran Is a Land of Mountains and Deserts 4

The Climate Is Diverse 6

Iran Is an Ancient Country 8

The Government Is a Theocratic Republic 10

Oil Production Drives the Economy 12

Public Education Is Free 14

Iran Is Taking Big Steps in Science and Technology 16

The Infrastructure Needs Work 18

The Population Is a Mix of Ethnic Groups 20

The Culture Is Shaped by Islam 22

Iran Tries to Provide Health Care for Everyone 24

Iranians Are Moving to Cities 26

Iran at a Glance 28

Where in the World? 29

Glossary 30

For More Information 31

Index 32

About the Author 32

Iran Is a Land of Mountains and Deserts

Iran is the second-largest country in the Middle East. It is the eighteenth-largest country in the world. Its total area is 636,371 square miles (1,648,195 sq km). Iran is nearly the size of the US state of Alaska.

Iran shares borders with Turkmenistan, Afghanistan, Pakistan, Iraq, Turkey, Armenia, and Azerbaijan. The Caspian Sea is to the north. The Persian Gulf and the Gulf of Oman are to the south.

Iran has rugged mountain chains and large deserts. The Zagros Mountains stretch from the northwest to the southeast. The Alborz Mountains run along the edge of the Caspian Sea. Iran's highest peak is Mount Damavand. It rises 18,934 feet (5,771 m). Mountain chains surround basins on a central plateau. To the east of the plateau are large deserts. The country also has dense forests, rainforests, and jungles.

Most of Iran's people live in the north and west. There the land is fertile and the temperatures are moderate. The central and eastern parts of Iran are the least populated.

Mount Damavand is a volcano that last erupted about 7,300 years ago.

The one road that crosses the Lut Desert is 180 miles (290 km) long.

THE HOTTEST SPOT ON EARTH?

Iran's Lut Desert has dunes, dust storms, and strange rock formations. Almost nothing grows there. But insects, reptiles, and desert foxes are seen. One day in 2005, the ground temperature reached 159.3 degrees Fahrenheit (70.7°C). It was recorded by a NASA satellite. The Lut is not the hottest spot on Earth every year. But that is still the hottest ground temperature on record.

30,000

Size in square miles (77,600 sq km) of Dasht-e Kavir, Iran's largest desert.

- Iran has mountain ranges, basins, deserts, and forests.
- Mount Damavand is the highest point.
- Most people live in the northern and western parts of the country.

The Climate Is Diverse

Much of Iran is hot and dry. But the country is large, and the climate varies. Winter in the northwest is cold and snowy. Temperatures drop to below freezing. Summers in the south are very hot. Daily temperatures can soar over 100 degrees Fahrenheit (38°C). There is not much rain. In most of the country, the annual rainfall is only about 9 inches (228 mm). More rain falls in the mountain valleys and along the coast of the Caspian Sea.

Most animals live in the wooded mountain regions and the central plateau. Brown bears, wild boars, and wolves make their homes in the forests. Deer, gazelles, and jackals are found on the plateau. Many trees have been cut down for lumber and fuel. Several animal and plant species are endangered. The Asiatic cheetah is critically endangered. The Persian leopard is endangered. The Caspian tiger is extinct.

More than 2,000 plant species grow in the forested areas and the plateau. In the spring, wild shrubs and plants provide food for many animals. Aquatic birds such as seagulls live near the coasts. Hundreds of varieties of fish are found in the Persian Gulf.

Less than 7 percent of Iran is forest.

The endangered Asiatic cheetah is known for the black "tear marks" in its fur.

40

Estimated number of Asiatic cheetahs in the wild in Iran, as of 2016.

- Iran is a large country with a diverse climate.
- Temperatures range from below freezing to above 100 degrees Fahrenheit (38°C).
- Deforestation has destroyed some animal and plant habitats.
- The coasts are home to many birds.

LITTLE AFRICA

Iran has many national parks and protected areas. Kavir National Park in the north is one. It is 1 million acres (404,685 hectares) of protected ecological zone. Only about 6 inches of rain (150 mm) fall each year. The park is known as Little Africa. Much of its wildlife is similar to what you would see on safari. Many animals in the park are endangered.

Iran Is an Ancient Country

Long before Iran was called Iran, it was known as Persia. Its civilization dates back thousands of years. It was ruled by dynasties of kings who were later called shahs. Susa was its first great city. People lived there as far back as 4200 BCE.

The Persian Empire was formed around 550 BCE. At its peak, its borders reached from the Mediterranean Sea to modern-day Pakistan. During the seventh century CE, Persia became part of the Islamic Empire. Islam became the official religion in 1501, when the Safavid dynasty took control.

In 1935, the country's name was changed to Iran. In 1941, Mohammad Reza Pahlavi became shah. He ruled Iran for 36 years. He tried to modernize and westernize the country. But Iran's religious leaders disagreed

Shah Mohammad Reza Pahlavi left Iran in 1979 and was granted asylum in Egypt.

with his plan. So did many of the people. Led by Ayatollah Khomeini, they started a revolution. Khomeini was a powerful religious leader. He had been living in exile for going against the shah.

In 1979, Pahlavi and his family fled Iran. Shortly after, Khomeini returned home. Iran became the Islamic Republic of Iran. Khomeini was its supreme leader. Later that year, Islamic students stormed the

American embassy in Tehran, the capital city. They took 52 Americans hostage. They didn't let them go for more than 400 days. Relations between the United States and Iran have been tense ever since.

Today Iran has uneasy relations with much of the world. The country has been working on a nuclear program. It has been accused of many human rights violations. Other countries and the United Nations have tried to change Iran's behavior with sanctions.

$20 billion

Estimated fortune of the Pahlavi family when they left Iran, in 1979 dollars.

- Iran was known as Persia until 1935.
- It was ruled by dynasties for thousands of years.
- Islam became the state religion in 1501.
- Iran became a republic in 1979.

TIMELINE

Around 550 BCE: Persian Empire is formed.

663 CE: Arab invasion begins.

1501: Start of the Safavid Empire.

1906: Iran adopts a constitution.

1925: Reza Khan becomes ruler of Persia.

1935: Persia is renamed Iran.

1941: Mohammad Reza Pahlavi becomes Shah of Iran.

1979: Islamic Revolution sends Pahlavi into exile. Iran becomes a republic. It adopts a new constitution.

1980: War between Iran and Iraq begins. It lasts eight years.

The Government Is a Theocratic Republic

Iran has been a theocratic republic since 1979. Some leaders are elected. Some are appointed. But there is no separation of church and state. Religious rules and beliefs are part of politics in Iran.

The supreme leader is the head of state. He is appointed for life. Ayatollah Ali Khamenei has been supreme leader since 1989. An ayatollah is a Shiite Muslim religious leader. Khamenei was appointed by the Assembly of Experts. This is a group of 88 Shiite religious leaders. They also guide the supreme leader.

The president is elected by the people. He is second-in-command to the supreme leader. He can only serve two four-year terms in a row. The president is guided by the Council of Ministers. Hassan Rouhani has been president of Iran since 2013.

There are two other decision-making groups in Iran. One is the Majlis, or the Parliament. Its 290 members are elected every four years. The other is the Guardian Council. This is Iran's most important decision-making body. It has 12 members. Six are appointed by the supreme leader. They are experts

Hassan Rouhani was reelected president in 2017 with 57 percent of the vote.

in Islamic law. Six are elected by the Majlis. They are experts in other areas of law.

Iran's military has two branches. They are the Regular Forces and the Islamic Revolutionary Guard Corps (IRGC). Both branches have the same general commander. Army commanders are appointed by the supreme leader.

All men in Iran must join the military when they turn 18. They must serve for 18 months.

46 million

Estimated number of Iranians who are eligible to vote.

- Iran has both elected and appointed leaders.
- The president is elected by the people.
- The Parliament and the Guardian Council are the decision-making bodies.
- All Iranian men must serve in the military starting at age 18.

Oil Production Drives the Economy

Iran's economy ranks nineteenth in the world for its gross domestic product (GDP). This is the total value of all goods a country produces in a year. In 2017, Iran's GDP was approximately $1.6 trillion.

Iran's economy has three parts. The state sector controls all large industries, such as foreign trade and banking. The cooperative sector includes companies that control production and distribution of products. The private sector covers the agricultural, animal, and service industries.

Iran's economy depends on energy. Iran is one of the top 10 oil producers in the world. In 2017, Iran exported nearly 1 billion barrels of oil. The country also exports plastics, chemicals, and fruit. Coal, copper, zinc, and gold are mined. Some goods Iran imports are cereals, machinery, and steel.

For many years, sanctions related to Iran's nuclear

Iran is working to boost its oil refinery capacity. It wants to be less reliant on imported fuels like gasoline.

Iran's currency is the Iranian Rial.

program blocked trade or froze assets. Some sanctions meant Iran couldn't make money from oil exports. This hurt the country's economy. When the sanctions were lifted, the economy boomed. In 2018, oil prices are low. Iran is making less money from exports. This limits investment to their economy. Unemployment is high, especially for young people. So people are going elsewhere for jobs. It's estimated that more than 150,000 educated Iranians leave the country every year.

30.5 million
Estimated number of workers in Iran in 2017.

- Iran is one of the top 10 oil producers in the world.
- The economy of Iran relies mostly on energy exports.
- Iran mines minerals such as gold and copper.

THINK ABOUT IT

What industries are important in your town? Which companies contribute to your local economy? How do they contribute?

6

Public Education Is Free

Iran spends 2.9 percent of its GDP on education. The government controls education through the Ministry of Education. Educational policies are passed by the Supreme Council of Education. Iran is divided into 31 provinces. Local governments control education in the provinces.

All children must attend primary school. Schools are single-sex. Boys go to boys' schools. Girls go to girls' schools. Primary education is free through eighth grade. After that, students can choose to attend free secondary education for three years. Students take exit exams to graduate. If they want to go to a free university, they take more exams. These can be difficult and competitive.

Men and women can be classmates at universities. Private

Muslim dress code requires females 13 and older to wear the hijab.

Boys line up to begin middle school in Tehran.

schools and universities exist in Iran. But they are expensive.

After the Islamic Revolution of 1979, schools in Iran changed. Textbooks were rewritten. Universities were closed from 1980–1983.

Curriculums and learning materials were made more Islamic. Western influences were purged.

Today most people in Iran over age 15 can read and write. Iran has a literacy rate of approximately 98 percent.

15 million

Approximate number of students in primary and secondary education in Iran.

- Children must attend school through eighth grade.
- Primary and secondary schools are single-sex.
- Textbooks were rewritten after the Islamic Revolution.

IRAN'S OLDEST MODERN UNIVERSITY

Tehran is Iran's capital city. The University of Tehran was started there in 1934. It ranks among the top 400 universities in the world. Over 55,000 students attend each year. The university is known for excellence in science and technology. It has also been a site of historical change. The Islamic Revolution of 1979 began at its front gates.

Iran Is Taking Big Steps in Science and Technology

Iran is one of the fastest-growing countries for scientific advancements. The Ministry of Science, Research, and Technology (MSRT) oversees and funds research. Most research is done at universities. The Amirkabir University of Technology is in Tehran, Iran's capital city. It ranks among the top 500 universities in the world.

The University of Tehran has been the site of major medical breakthroughs and discoveries. The first heart and lung transplants performed in Iran were done there.

Iran ranks twenty-first in the world for biotechnology research. In 2014, its scientists published 3,957 scientific articles about biotechnology. Iran is working hard on nanotechnology.

One of Iran's most important institutes is IROST. This stands for the Iranian Research Organization for Science and Technology.

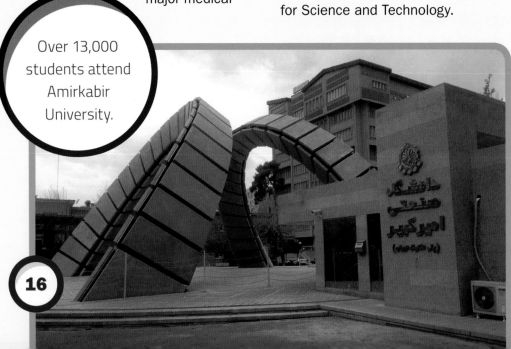

Over 13,000 students attend Amirkabir University.

Iran has produced the most nanotechnology publications of all Islamic countries.

IROST was founded in 1980, right after the Islamic Revolution. It supports developing technologies in agriculture, biology, chemistry, and mechanics.

Much of Iran's scientific research focuses on nuclear energy. Other countries have tried to stop this research. They don't want Iran to develop nuclear weapons. In 2016, Iran agreed to perform nuclear research only for peaceful purposes. But concerns about Iran's nuclear weapons capability remain.

46
Number of organ transplant centers in Iran.

- The Ministry of Science, Research, and Technology funds research.
- The University of Tehran performs heart and lung transplants.
- Iran performs a lot of nuclear energy research.

THINK ABOUT IT

Iran is growing because it is investing in science and technology. How do science and technology help the community where you live? What type of science or technology interests you the most? Why?

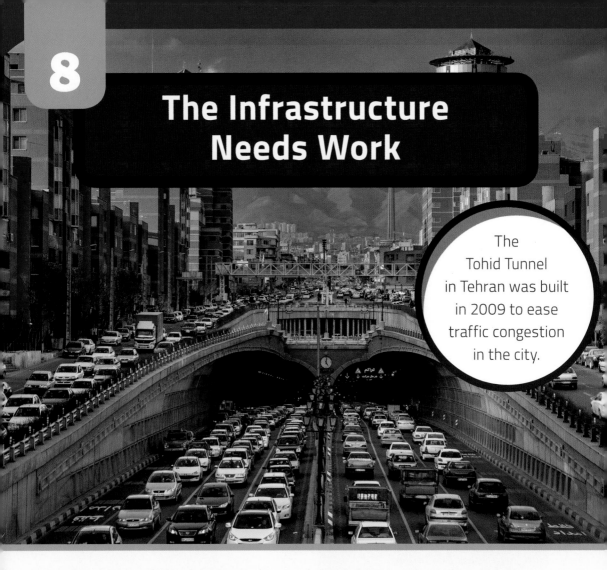

The Infrastructure Needs Work

The Tohid Tunnel in Tehran was built in 2009 to ease traffic congestion in the city.

Iran has nearly 124,000 miles (200,000 km) of roads. Many of these roads need upgrading. Approximately 23,900 miles (38,463 km) are unpaved.

The capital city, Tehran, is home to 8.8 million people. Millions more commute into the city for work. Constructing roadways in this crowded city isn't easy. The

Sadr Expressway, built in 2012, was Iran's first multilevel, two-lane expressway. Today city officials think the expressway made traffic worse, not better. More than 4 million cars clog Tehran's roads. More public transportation is needed.

Iran has not been able to maintain its airplanes and airports. Flying capacity is only 6 million passengers

The Tehran Metro System has only eight operating lines.

a year. Nearby countries, such as Dubai, fly 78 million passengers a year. Iran has one of the oldest passenger fleets in the world. Many of its planes are aging Russian jets.

Railways have been neglected for years. Iran plans to invest 1 percent of the money it makes from oil exports to repair its rail lines. By 2025, it aims to add 6,214 miles (10,000 km) of new lines.

Iran is rapidly developing communication technologies. These will help improve the economy. The country has invested in fiber optic, mobile, and satellite services. People can communicate and do business more easily. Wi-Fi is available in most cities. Internet service extends into many rural areas.

319
Number of airports in Iran.

- Building and repairing roads in heavily populated areas is difficult.
- By 2025, Iran aims to add 6,214 miles (10,000 km) to its railway system.
- Communication technologies allow Iranians to be more productive.

THINK ABOUT IT

What are some major roads near you? Is there a lot of traffic where you live? How long does it take you to get to school on a normal day?

19

The Population Is a Mix of Ethnic Groups

Iran's population is the seventeenth largest in the world. More than 82 million people live there. The average household size is getting smaller. It decreased from 4.9

96

Estimated number of ethnic tribes in Iran.

- Families in Iran are getting smaller.
- The population is made up of several ethnic groups.
- Over 1 million nomads live in Iran.
- Farsi is the official language.

members in 1992 to 3.3 today. Families are having fewer children. It's also becoming more acceptable to remain single and live alone.

Iranian society is made up of six major ethnic groups. They are the Baloch, Azerbaijani Turks, Arabs, Kurds, Lurs, and Turkmans. These groups have been living in Iran for centuries. They occupy different regions

Iranian families are smaller today.

of the country and speak their own languages.

There are also nomads from other ethnic backgrounds. These groups depend on raising animals to survive. They move with the changing seasons. They often migrate to flee political unrest. Most nomadic groups are organized like tribes. Over 1 million nomads live in Iran today.

The majority of Iran's people are ethnically Persian. They make up approximately 65 percent of the population, more than 53 million people. The largest ethnic minority is the Azerbaijani Turks. They make up about 16 percent of the population, more than 13 million people. Almost all Iranians are Muslim. Some 90 to 95 percent are Shiite Muslims. The rest are Sunni Muslims.

Persian, also known as Farsi, is the official language spoken. However, many dialects are used. Schools also teach English, French, and other languages.

Kurdish people have lived in northwestern Iran for centuries.

10

The Culture Is Shaped by Islam

Muslims from all over the world gather to pray as part of their pilgrimage to Mecca.

Almost everyone in Iran is Muslim. Islam has been the official religion since the start of the sixteenth century. Two major branches of Islam are the Sunni and the Shia. Most Muslims in Iran belong to the Shia branch.

Each year, about 2 million Muslims go on a pilgrimage to Mecca in Saudi Arabia. This is the holiest city of Islam. The pilgrimage is called the hajj. Every Muslim is required to perform the hajj at least once in their lifetime.

Another important religious holiday is Ramadan. Every day for a month, Muslims fast from dawn to dusk. They get up early to eat before dawn. They don't eat again until sundown.

Hospitality is important in Iran. Meals are often shared with extended family. Pistachios, almonds, and saffron are used in many dishes. Pomegranates and other fruits are favorites. Lamb, chicken, and beef kebabs are popular. No meal is complete without sabzi khordan, a plate of fresh herbs. Mint, tarragon, basil, and cilantro are mixed with nuts and cheese. Alcohol has been illegal in Iran since the Islamic Revolution.

Women in Iran made progress when the Pahlavis were shahs. They gained the right to vote and run for office. They became diplomats, judges, and police officers. Six women were elected to Iran's Parliament. The Family Protection Law of 1975 gave women equal rights in marriage and divorce. But things changed quickly after the revolution. Today women's rights in Iran are strictly limited. Women can't even watch men's sports in stadiums.

110,000
Tons of dried tea consumed in Iran every year.

- Almost all people in Iran are Shiite Muslims.
- All Muslims must perform the hajj at least once.
- Ramadan lasts for a whole month.
- Women's rights were severely limited after the Islamic Revolution.

In March 2018, 35 women were arrested for trying to sneak into a soccer match.

Meals often include sabzi khordan. Tea is enjoyed throughout the day.

23

Iran Tries to Provide Health Care for Everyone

Iran spends 7 percent of its GDP on health services. The constitution guarantees basic health care for all citizens. In 2014, Iran began to reform its health care system. It is overseen by the Ministry of Health. Not all health care is free. However, much of the cost is paid for by the government.

Iran's health care system is improving. But it also has some problems. Sanctions have made it hard to import medicines and supplies for patients. Cities struggle to provide care for their fast-growing populations. Private hospitals and clinics exist, but they are expensive. Many people can't afford them.

Rural communities have limited technology and services. Skilled doctors are in short supply in these areas. Most villages have a Health House. These are run by community health workers and volunteers. So most rural people have access to basic health services.

More skilled doctors are needed in Iran.

Iran faces health challenges. Leading health problems include heart disease and diabetes. Many people smoke and have diets rich in fried foods. Obesity affects 26 percent of the population. The average life expectancy in Iran is 76 years.

Private hospitals often have the most advanced medical equipment.

ROUHANICARE

In 2014, President Hassan Rouhani introduced *Tarh-e Salaamat*, a new government health plan. This program was a step toward universal health care. It was nicknamed Rouhanicare, like Obamacare in the United States. Today 550 of Iran's 900 hospitals are run by the state. Access to services and quality care is difficult in certain areas. More government funding is needed. But many more Iranians are now able to get the treatment they need.

1.5
Average number of doctors for every 1,000 Iranians.

- The Ministry of Health manages public hospitals in Iran.
- Health Houses run by community health workers and volunteers serve rural areas.
- Pharmacies have difficulty getting many life-saving medicines.

Iranians Are Moving to Cities

Tehran is the most populous city in Iran.

Iran is becoming more urban and less rural. Most people live in cities already. This number is increasing. Today young Iranians receive a better education. Cities offer more job opportunities. Fewer people are staying in rural areas. Water shortages make jobs such as farming more difficult. Half of all rural households in Iran live in poverty.

In the city, many people live in apartments. Wealthier Iranians live in luxurious high-rise buildings. Villas for the newly wealthy dot the foothills of Tehran. Homes in the suburbs are small but comfortable. These are typically made of metal and concrete.

People in rural areas often live with extended family. Each family has their own rooms. Kitchen space is shared. Rural houses are usually made with mud bricks.

Most homes in Iran have running water, electricity, and natural gas. Fossil fuels produce 83 percent of Iran's electricity.

74.4

Percent of Iran's population living in urban areas.

- Cities have better opportunities for educated Iranians.
- Fewer people are staying in rural villages.
- Iran has many dams to manage its water resources and generate electricity.

AN ANCIENT TRADITION CONTINUES

The oldest examples of Persian carpet weaving date back to the sixteenth century. Today Iran is famous for its hand-loomed carpets. These are prized possessions throughout the world. Carpet looms are found throughout the country. Each location has its own artistic pattern and style. Today carpet weaving is the most widespread and well-known art form in Iran.

Water is limited, so managing it is important. Iran has built 600 dams in the last 30 years. Fourteen percent of electricity is produced from hydroelectric power. In 2017, Iran opened its first wind farm. Energy from the 22 wind turbines produce another 15 percent of Iran's electricity.

The Dez Dam, one of the largest in Iran, provides power, and water for irrigation.

Iran at a Glance

Population in 2018: 82,011,735

Area: 636,371 square miles (1,648,195 sq km)

Capital: Tehran

Largest Cities: Tehran, Mashhad, Esfahan, Karaj, Shiraz

Flag:

National Language: Persian (Farsi)

Currency: Iranian Rial

What people who live in Iran are called: Iranians

Where in the World?

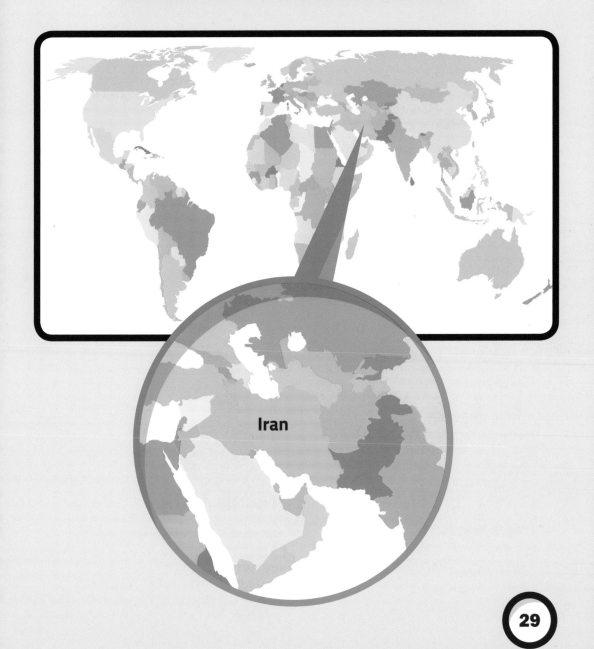

Iran

Glossary

basin
In geography, an area of land enclosed by hills and mountains. A basin can be a prairie or a desert.

biotechnology
Technology that uses living organisms to make chemicals and products or perform industrial tasks.

dynasty
A series of leaders from the same family or group.

endangered
An endangered animal is close to extinction. The species is in danger of dying out.

ethnic
Having to do with a particular race or culture. A group that shares a common and distinctive culture.

ethnic minority
A group that is different from a larger group in one or more ways. These might include race, language, culture, or religion. Ethnic minorities are often treated differently. They may experience discrimination.

freeze assets
To put a hold on the economic resources of a person, group, or country.

gross domestic product (GDP)
The total value of all goods a country produces in a year.

literacy
The ability to read and write.

nanotechnology
Technology that deals with the study and use of extremely small things.

nomads
Individuals or groups of people who live by traveling instead of settling in one place.

pilgrimage
A long journey, often made for a religious purpose to a sacred place.

sanction
An action taken to force a country to obey international laws. Examples are limiting trade or cutting off economic aid.

shah
A title given to the rulers of Iran, formerly Persia.

theocratic republic
A type of government that is based on following the rules of a certain religion.

westernize
To adopt ideas and ways of doing things that are common in North America and most of Europe.

For More Information

Books

Sheen, Barbara. *Growing Up in Iran.* Growing Up Around the World. San Diego, CA: Reference Point Press, 2018.

Steele, Philip. *Iran and the West.* Our World Divided. New York, NY: PowerKids Press, 2013.

Wilson, Rosie. *Discover Iran.* Discover Countries. New York, NY: PowerKids Press, 2012.

Simmons, Walter. *Iran.* Exploring Countries. Minnetonka, MN: Bellwether, 2011.

Visit 12StoryLibrary.com

Scan the code or use your school's login at **12StoryLibrary.com** for recent updates about this topic and a full digital version of this book. Enjoy free access to:

- Digital ebook
- Breaking news updates
- Live content feeds
- Videos, interactive maps, and graphics
- Additional web resources

Note to educators: Visit 12StoryLibrary.com/register to sign up for free premium website access. Enjoy live content plus a full digital version of every 12-Story Library book you own for every student at your school.

Index

animals, 6-7, 21
Ayatollah Ali Khamenei, 10
Ayatollah Khomeini, 8

Caspian tiger, 6
cheetah, 6-7

deforestation, 7

energy, 12-13, 17, 27
equal rights, 23
exports, 12-13, 19

Farsi language, 20-21, 28
foods, 22, 25
fossil fuels, 26

gross domestic product (GDP), 12, 14, 24, 30

human rights violations, 9

Iraq, 4, 9
Islam, 8-9, 22
Islamic Empire, 8

literacy, 15, 30
Lut Desert, 5

Mecca, 22
military, 11
Mount Damavand, 4-5
Muslims, 21, 22-23

nomads, 20-21, 30
nuclear program, 9, 12

Persian carpets, 27
Persian Empire, 8-9
Persian Gulf, 4, 6

pilgrimage, 22, 30
poverty, 26

religion , 8, 22, 30
revolution, 8-9, 15, 17, 23
Rouhan, Hassani, 4

sanctions, 9, 12-13, 24
Shah Mohammad Reza Pahlavi, 8-9

Tehran, 9, 15, 16-17, 18-19, 26, 28
temperature, 4-5, 6
transportation, 18

United States, 9, 25

water shortages, 26-27

About the Author

Danielle Sovereign is a graduate of St. Olaf College with degrees in English and French. She enjoys researching and writing nonfiction books, as well as writing fiction for competitions. She lives in Chicago with her family.

READ MORE FROM 12-STORY LIBRARY

Every 12-Story Library Book is available in many fomats. For more information, visit 12StoryLibrary.com